Dear Parent:

Your child's love of reading starts here!

Every child learns to read in a different way and at his or her own speed. Some go back and forth between reading levels and read favorite books again and again. Others read through each level in order. You can help your young reader improve and become more confident by encouraging his or her own interests and abilities. From books your child reads with you to the first books he or she reads alone, there are I Can Read Books for every stage of reading:

SHARED READING
Basic language, word repetition, and whimsical illustrations, ideal for sharing with your emergent reader

BEGINNING READING
Short sentences, familiar words, and simple concepts for children eager to read on their own

READING WITH HELP
Engaging stories, longer sentences, and language play for developing readers

READING ALONE
Complex plots, challenging vocabulary, and high-interest topics for the independent reader

I Can Read Books have introduced children to the joy of reading since 1957. Featuring award-winning authors and illustrators and a fabulous cast of beloved characters, I Can Read Books set the standard for beginning readers.

A lifetime of discovery begins with the magical words "I Can Read!"

Visit www.icanread.com for information
on enriching your child's reading experience.

This book is just for 'roo!

—J.B.

The National Wildlife Federation & Ranger Rick contributors: Children's
Publication Staff, Licensing Staff, and in-house naturalist David Mizejewski

Ranger Rick: I Wish I Was a Kangaroo
Copyright © 2021 National Wildlife Federation
All rights reserved.
Printed in the United States of America. No part of this book may be used or reproduced in any manner
whatsoever without written permission except in the case of brief quotations embodied in critical articles and
reviews. For information address HarperCollins Children's Books, a division of HarperCollins Publishers, 195
Broadway, New York, NY 10007.
www.icanread.com
www.RangerRick.com

Library of Congress Control Number: 2020949335
ISBN 978-0-06-243238-4 (trade bdg.) — ISBN 978-0-06-243237-7 (pbk.)

22 23 24 25 CWM 10 9 8 7 6 5 4 3   ❖   First Edition

I Can Read!

BEGINNING 1 READING

Ranger Rick

I Wish I Was a Kangaroo

by Jennifer Bové

HARPER

An Imprint of HarperCollinsPublishers

What if you wished

you were a kangaroo?

Then you became a young kangaroo.

Could you eat like a kangaroo?

Move like a kangaroo?

Live in a kangaroo family?

And would you want to? Find out!

Where would you live?

There are many different kinds

of kangaroos.

They live in Australia

and on the island of Papua New Guinea.

Kangaroos live in grassy areas,
on rocky slopes, and in forests.
Some even live up in trees.

All kangaroos have long tails
and long back feet.
Some kinds of kangaroos are big.
They can be over six feet tall!

Small kangaroos, called wallabies, are less than three feet tall.

Are you taller than a wallaby?

How would your life begin?

All newborn kangaroos
are smaller than your finger.
They have no fur at all.

Baby kangaroos are called joeys.
A joey lives in a pocket of skin
on its mother's belly.
The pocket is called a pouch.

A joey stays warm and safe
in its mother's pouch for months.
As the joey grows bigger,
it grows fur.

Soon, the joey can peek out.
When it is ready, the joey
climbs out of the pouch.

**How would you learn
to be a kangaroo?**

When a joey leaves its mom's pouch,
it starts exploring and playing.
Joeys play with their moms.
They practice hopping
on their big back feet
like grown-up kangaroos.

Do you like to hop?

14

What would your family be like?

Kangaroos live in groups

called mobs.

A mob can have just a few kangaroos or it can have hundreds.

How would you talk?

Kangaroos are mostly quiet animals. They sniff each other to say, "Hi!" Mother kangaroos make soft clucks to their joeys.

Kangaroos stomp their feet loudly
to tell others when danger is near.

What would you eat?

Different kinds of kangaroos
eat different things.
Some are grazers that eat grass.

Other kinds of kangaroos are browsers that eat leaves and twigs.

How would you stay clean?

Kangaroos have special claws on their back feet.

Kangaroos use these claws

to comb bugs out of their fur.

Where would you sleep?

Some kangaroos dig beds in the soil.

Some snuggle on rocks to sleep.

Tree kangaroos sleep on tree branches.

Joeys nap in their moms' pouches.

Most kangaroos sleep during the day and stay awake at night.

How would growing up change you?

As joeys grow up, they grow brave.

They don't stay close to their moms.

Males wrestle and kick

to see who is strongest.

Females find food together.

At about two years old,

joeys are full-grown kangaroos!

Being a kangaroo could be cool.

But do you want to hop on big feet?

Grow up in a pouch?

Eat grass or twigs?

Luckily, you don't have to.

You're not a kangaroo.

You're YOU!

Did You Know?

🐾 Kangaroos are great swimmers.

🐾 Kangaroos are fast. They can hop at speeds up to forty miles per hour.

🐾 Male kangaroos are called jacks. Females are called jills.

🐾 Animals that carry their babies in pouches are called marsupials (mar-soo-pee-als). Kangaroos, opossums, and koalas are marsupials.

Kangaroos are super jumpers.
Large kangaroos can leap thirty feet forward!
How far can you jump? Find out!

In a big room or your yard, mark a starting line
with tape.

Stand on the starting line and hold a tape
measure. Ask a parent or friend to pull the tape
measure until it reaches thirty feet.

Mark the 30-foot line with tape.

Take turns standing on the starting line and
jumping forward on both feet.

Measure and write down how many feet each
person jumps.

Math Challenge: Subtract each player's jumping
distance from the kangaroo's distance. How
much farther can a kangaroo jump than you?

Wild Words

Browser: an animal that eats leaves and twigs

Grazer: an animal that eats grass

Joey: a baby kangaroo

Kangaroo: a mammal that has big back feet and a long tail

Mob: a group of kangaroos

Pouch: a pocket of skin on a mother kangaroo's belly where she carries her joey

Wallaby: the name for small kangaroos

Dig Deeper
WANT TO FIND OUT EVEN MORE ABOUT KANGAROOS?

Check out the Ranger Rick website:
www.RangerRick.com
SEARCH: kangaroo

Photography © Getty Images by Lea Scaddan, Saikat Saha, Freder, Mollypix, Jamie Lamb-elusive-images.co.uk, Burroblando, Michelle Page, Artush, Vicki Smith, Andrew Haysom, Tobias Titz, Oxime, Jami Tarris, Nick Rains, Southern Lightscapes-Australia, Npoizit, MaZiKab, Trek13, Mark Newman, Photogerson